THREADS *of* RESILIENCE

Threads of Resilience

Copyright © 2023 by Tethered Wrds.

All rights reserved. No part of this book may be reproduced in any form without permission in writing from the copyright owner, except in the case of brief quotations included in critical reviews and certain other noncommercial uses permitted by copyright law.

Book design by Elizabeth Bell

ISBN: 979-8-9892453-0-7
Library of Congress Control Number: 2023918751

For inquiries, please contact
Tethered Wrds at *connect@tetheredwrds.com*

THREADS *of* RESILIENCE

WEAVING THE HUMAN SPIRIT THROUGH POETRY

PROSE & POETRY BY **TETHERED WRDS**

CONTENTS

viii	Introduction
01	Journey

PART ONE

06	The Promised Land
08	Reflected Glory
10	History Repeated
12	When Worlds Collide: Thoughts on the Americas
14	Another World
16	Facing the Elements
22	The Hill
24	Bodies
26	Pay Up
28	The Aves
30	Settings
32	Rejected
34	Recounting
38	Yeimy (Jamie)
40	Proof
42	Overwhelmed
44	Self Destruction
46	Untitled
48	Drained

50	Hospitality
52	Pieces of my Heart
54	Marked
58	Give me a Break
60	Filled
62	Underfoot
64	Untitled
66	Corriendo
68	A Gentle Soul
72	A Power House
80	Let Freedom Ring
82	Pensive
84	Consequences
86	Trigger Warning
90	Idols
92	Divine Flex
98	Today is the Day
102	Remnants
104	Prayer Language
106	"Bless Your Heart"

PART TWO

111	Beauty Heals
115	Para Jason
119	Arrogance
120	I'm Yelling in this Next One…

125	Inheritance
126	Historias
127	A Lone Star Conversation
131	Huracån
132	Exchanges
133	The Hondurian
137	Gifted
138	Jugo
141	Lemonade
145	Question
146	Would We Commit?
147	Dog & Horse Show
148	Adventure & Risk
149	The Roar of Heaven
150	Treasured Tales
151	Santa Muerte
152	Witness
155	Mirando
156	Distance
157	Always Near
159	Peace be with You & Peace I Leave with You
162	My Final Report
166	Shot on iPhone
172	Acknowledgments

INTRODUCTION

This was my first trip to the Southern Border and little did I know many more would follow. My book of choice was *Latino Americans: The 500 year legacy that shaped a nation* by Ray Suarez, the person I traveled with, a stranger. Here I am flying with a stranger to meet strangers from distant lands: Charleston, SC to Matamoras, MX. As I read of our American history and traversed my country to learn of others' potential mark on our history, I could only capture my journey and the narratives of migrants in the form of poetry. The weight of what I would experience and encounter over the next few years could only be digested through this art form.

So you understand the political climate; my first trip was during Trump's Presidency, MPP (Migrant Protection Protocol or the Remain in Mexico Policy) was in place then Title 42 was implemented because of the pandemic and this continued under Biden, my travels were 2020-2023.

The narratives I share, the stories I've captured and the information intertwined in this art-form is real, raw and in many regards can be a trigger to which I've added a warning on page 86 for that poem. What is written and shared has been told to me with the confidence and understanding that I would amplify migrant voices.

My hope is to help change the narrative around immigration, asylum-seekers, refugees, "illegals" or those undocumented. I hope to inspire dignity for them but also in you and that by these words you will take the courageous step of vulnerability. Would you settle in to understand the narrative of a stranger and allow your spirit to be weaved into the tapestry of humanity, for the common good, for a change in worldview?

A WORD:

In part one, what you'll find laid out before each poem is "a word" or "brief" as to where I was, what I was thinking or what influenced that poem. In part two, I release your imagination so each poem speaks freely.

Here is my journey

in the form of spilled ink.

JOURNEY

Journey with me.
Let me take your mind's eye across
land, lakes & silver tone light rays of the sun.
See the landscape shift
when you trek miles
to meet those who have trekked miles
to be met with walls & arms
not of embrace but fire power.
Dust clouds turned up
by propeller winds meeting desert floors,
Border Patrol use helicopters
to turn away those
who should have made different choices.
Water washing over your body
as you cross bodies of water
the only borders
carved by God's own hand.
It seems this land was not made
for you and me,
it was made for those
we have decided to keep
those we deem worthy
of bearing our citizenship
or at least those that can pay for it.

JOURNEY

You may not be ready for this journey
and I assure you that it is hard
but I've got stories
of brown beauties;
babies, toddlers,
preteens, mothers,
fathers that have walked the distance
seeking a life
that would make a difference,
maybe for themselves
but mostly for their children
and in their mind's eye
their resolve understands all the more
that the risk will never outweigh the reward.
—
"How hard must life be
  for a chance to live like me?"

PART

ONE

I thought of my faith and the impact I could leave on this world. Why my faith has led me to this current journey and path of service for others through immigration. As I read the scriptures, I was reminded that this isn't our world yet we are to redeem all we can to the glory of God and to live in hope as we travel through meaning we are sojourners.

THE PROMISED LAND
CHS → MFE

Could it be
that the immigrant narrative
is a physical reminder
of the saved sojourners story—
people of an upside down kingdom?

Jesus tells us to care for the foreigners
he shares that,
"the first shall be last & the last shall be first".
So I look at the immigrant & see myself;
a citizen of Heaven
passing through the Kingdom of Earth,
interacting with her citizens;
knowing full well my journey
will soon come to an end.
All I want is to be loved,
cared for, shown mercy & grace
all while enjoying
the unknown adventure,
treacherous at times but treasured
for eternity
because like the immigrant,
I too hope for
The Promised Land.

Certainly, there is something to be learned, understood and felt when we sit back and read our history. The human heart and our natural condition are bent on self. So when we strive to do better, to be better on behalf of the common good, if it's not tethered to an awareness and understanding of where we came from then no change will be made. I praise God for the changes we have made & changes we will continue to make. Flying over the gulf with the sun reflecting silver linings off the water, the chapters I read in Ray Suarez's book reflected where we came from with a broken heart.

REFLECTED GLORY
FLYING INTO IAH

The sun glistens
off what looks like silver deposits
in the Earth's veins.
If only the Spanish Conquistadors
knew that their conquest for
gold & silver
were the stories & kinship based on our
indigenous brothers & sister's dreams.
They were gifted glimpses
of this rich land—
aerial views through astral projections
as they sat 'round campfires
and told of the connections to
lakes, rivers,
channels & marshes
reflecting Glory!

I connected the dots of indigenous people in our history and those crossing our borders. I look out over creation: one globe, one world, *separate people*. We have a problem of always treating brown skinned beauties differently.

HISTORY REPEATED
FLYING INTO MFE

the vastness of your creation
the masses of your creatures
spread across the Earth.
I sit in this mechanical bird
chasing the sun,
moving backwards in time
yet not fast or far enough in history
to warn our fore-fathers
of the disastrous forbidden fruit.
yet,
had I the chance I know how it plays out
cause if they didn't heed the word of God.
why would they heed the word of man?

If you've traveled South definitely to the South-West and West Coast, it quickly becomes apparent that we are a diverse nation. It may be a *"duh"* statement, I know, but does it resonate that our diversity has strong Latino and Spanish ties? We learn of Plymouth Rock, the pilgrims, John Smith and Pocahontas. We know and are taught of the Mayflower and Charles Towne landings but 50 years prior, Spanish blood met indigenous and Central American faces on these native lands.

WHEN WORLDS COLLIDE: THOUGHTS ON THE AMERICAS
SOMEWHERE OVER TX

Two worlds collide,
English & Spanish.
neighbors across the sea,
rivals on the land of the free.
Here I am,
traveling through a land of immigrants
who bear the name of
South, Central & North American
but only my rights
hold any merit
as a natural-born citizen.
What they don't teach you
is the history of the Spaniards
ruling over the Hispanic & Indigenous.
This isn't a praise moment of history,
it's just interesting
that we push back
on brown skinned non-English speakers
yet live in cities & states
named after Spanish-speaking people.

I was exhausted from traveling. It was late and the person picking us up, someone I had yet to meet, was late. The air was still, with no other souls outside of us outsiders. I knew I wasn't in Charleston anymore. Hell, I knew I wasn't in the southeast anymore! There was a different vibe here.

ANOTHER WORLD
MCALLEN AIRPORT

A radio plays in the distance
sounds like its got
tin can speakers.
I feel like
I'm in an episode of breaking bad—
arid air.
No one in sight
the sandstone sun worn facade
of this small airport
has seen better days.

These borderlands could be backdrops for something out of Hollywood, definitely a Netflix series. Is this America? Faded, rugged buildings, a solemn filter hit the scene though the sun shone. I mean, the liquor store was out of business! The exchange of bodies were purposeful, intentional transactions, both for the Americans and Mexicans. There was a dystopian type of freedom palpable to a few.

FACING THE ELEMENTS
THE INTERNATIONAL BRIDGE

Barbed wire,
bare walls,
steel slats to allow
the coming & going
of the wind—
F R E E D O M !
but only for certain elements.

Hours turned into days

once I crossed the international bridge, life changed.

ON THE INTERNATIONAL BRIDGE LOOKING ACROSS AT THE AMERICAN WALKWAY

They gifted me their trust and narratives. My five senses allowed me a glimpse into their experience at this camp—their world—but I could never fully know or walk in their shoes. We walked the bank of the Rio Grande and while under a tree looked out about a football field's distance across a natural border into the land of the United States of America: fences, buildings and a white tent atop the embankment. This was the immigration courts, beheld and out of reach, especially during the year 2020 when the world was under quarantine.

THE HILL
ON THE BANKS OF THE RIO GRANDE

The beacon of hope
is a white peak
atop a hill of green reeds
yet,
most people
will never make it.
Their stories
are lost in translation
screams snared
by Rio Grande winds.

I'm all for protecting our borders and our people, that isn't the issue at hand, nor am I screaming, "Open borders! No rule of law!" Order, Law, Protection, Service—all these morals and principles of life excellence—stem from a good God. As a man of faith, I hold to the scriptures, tethered to the words of Jesus and not just the red letters. As I understand, Jesus fulfilled and embodied full truth and grace so I thought to myself, how would he serve and protect? How would Jesus keep order and protect the sojourner? I truly believe there is an answer but what we have been doing isn't it. I look at my country of origin, my home, and feel sick to my stomach.

America, will you keep your promises?

BODIES
THE RIO GRANDE

On the banks of the Rio Grande
your name is laughable—
but
it's not the body of water we speak of
it's the bodies of persons
flowing over themselves
thirsty for our hopes & dreams.

Money runs the world. It's amazing what it can get you, bringing life and destruction. I laid eyes on papers and documents of many asylum seekers, from lawyers, notaries, translators being paid for cases to those they paid to guide them up to the border. Still, money can't seem to buy their freedom.

PAY UP
LOOKING OVER COURT DOCUMENTS
AND LISTENING TO STORIES

Asylum seekers on the bridge!
turn back... (*sigh*)
you don't have enough money.

This immigration camp was on the banks of the Rio Grande in Matamoros, Mexico, the counterpart of Brownsville, TX. The space used to be a park and is now occupied by tents, tarps and a few thousand people. It's an area of barbed wire fencing and the migrants live in these cages under all elements, inhumane conditions due to the Migrant Protection Protocol implemented by our government.

THE AVES
WALKING A DIRT PATH

I find it interesting
the only aves
to frequent the camp
are cowbirds.
Could it be
there's a familiarity
to herding cattle?

It was about lunch time and this was usually my favorite time. The food was always delicious: arepas, tortillas, rice and black beans. These women built stoves in the ground and set up makeshift kitchens and these moments around a meal allowed a fortification of community that almost made you forget the dire situation they lived in.

SETTINGS
LUNCHTIME

Royalty
is a table
set in an immigration camp.
You've never seen
sapphire blues so vibrant,
hunter greens so rich,
splashes of pantone yellows
—
and I'm just describing tents.

We met with a local pastor who takes in former gang members and youth. He serves faithfully at the southern border and in Matamoras, he's loved by many. I appreciated hearing his stories but due to his proximity to *"those people"* he also became pushed to the fringe from peers.

REJECTED
SOMEWHERE ACROSS THE BORDER

hip hop church
cartel youth
pastor in the wild
rejected.

Most of the migrants in Matamoros under MPP are women and children. It's amazing how resilient these kids and adolescents are. But I can't explain the joy and laughter that they found even in the hardship of it all. While many spirits were broken they all held on to the hope of something better and more out of life.

RECOUNTING
ON THE BANKS OF THE RIO GRANDE

tell me your story:
children recount
narratives & atrocities
innocence tainted
humanity stolen
forced to trade their youth
for a broken adult world.

OVERLOOKING THE RIO GRANDE FROM THE INTERNATIONAL BRIDGE

Yeimy, with her sister and mother, made the trek from El Salvador. This trio really became a leader in the camp. Yeimy had a sharp mind, a quick wit and knew how to hold her own even with the adults. I asked Yeimy what she'd like to do when she made it to the U.S. she said, "I'd love to serve in the military and become a general to lead others."

YEIMY (JAMIE)
FROM EL SALVADOR

valiant,
observant,
strength embodied;
she is eleven—
the force in the eyes of this fierce future
will be unstoppable.

Here's another for Yeimy. I heard her mom tell us numerous stories but I wanted to hear a specific narrative from Yeimy's perspective.

PROOF
UNDER THE CANOPY OF A HOT AUGUST DAY

She looked at me
from the corner of her eye,
sat back & kicked one foot up.
Bit her lip,
then shook her head
the silence told me everything.
All that was missing
were shots of whiskey
yet in that moment
I couldn't handle her proof.

When you step outside of yourself and lay down all that you know or think you know to embrace another, it's amazing how perspectives change. The stories and conditions of these people in Mexico—because of what my country enforced there—overwhelmed me. I will never un-know nor un-see. I was broken by the brokenness of our system and the injustices occurring. Aside from weeping, all I could do was keep writing.

OVERWHELMED
LOST IN THOUGHTS AND EMOTIONS

Emotions ran deep
as I processed the narratives
of these bronze bodied warriors.
My synapses & soul were overwhelmed
so I poured out the inkwell
as my eyes & heart overflowed.

I realized that borders and the defenses we set up truly just end up hurting humanity and the very nation we are trying to protect. Nothing in the makeup of border walls and angst builds health. The walls destroy landscapes, I've seen them destroy landmarks, land is taken or given for the sense of security when all that's needed is an embrace of humanity. If we are honest, border walls don't keep out bad people or evil, they are a false sense of security and end up only hurting those that actually need help and hurting relationships between persons because of the fear mentality.

SELF DESTRUCTION
AT THE BORDER WALL

Borders
yeah we got those.
Once again evil
twists divine words
and humanity falls
for lies.
God only set boundaries
for the waters
&
we destroy ourselves.

At some point, faith and life will meet face to face and we are called to submit not to our feelings or opinions, but to something greater, a more excellent way. I've seen, heard, argued with and blatantly witnessed too many people of faith, Christians, who speak one way and live totally different. I am not raising suspicions of hypocrisy but suspicions of whether or not we are truly being Christlike in kindness, friendship and love for others.

UNTITLED

I'm not the Christ
but be damn sure
I'm trying.

If you haven't picked up on it yet, I am a man of faith, broken as I may be—I love Jesus. The days were long and at one point I was spent on all fronts. I don't know where I was but I remember pausing.

DRAINED

I wonder if this is how Jesus felt
after a long day on his feet & a tired heart?

One night I decided with my two-person team that we would stay with the migrants, to sleep where they slept, to feel and hear what they felt and heard during the night. It was late and the camp had fallen asleep. My team and I had it in mind that we would post up against a tree on the banks of the Rio Grande. Well, someone woke up and notified Sandra that we had returned and they were not letting their guests sleep on the ground against a tree. So she woke some others and gathered a few items so we could rest as comfortably as we could. She embodied hospitality and care.

HOSPITALITY
MATAMOROS, MX

The Son of Man,
our Lord & King
didn't have a place to lay his head.
I'm ready to do the same
when a migrant walked out of the darkness
and lead me to a cot
under mosquito nets.

There's one other place in the world that stole a piece of my heart, Bolivia. Back in 2015 I visited an orphanage in the jungles. I'm reminded that "stranger" is only a brief title; for once you break bread, no longer are you speaking with nameless people, but persons who have made an impact on your life. People I've heard speak, laugh, cry and share frustrations. People drained by the same sun, the same stench reached our noses due to lack of care by authorities, these aren't strangers but friends—kin of global humanity.

PIECES OF MY HEART

faces to names
pedazos de mi corazón
exchanged once again

MARKED
A MOMENT & MEMORY OF MANAGED TENSION

I've witnessed foxes
tenderly carry daisies
across boundaries.
The care was unexpected,
their shrewd eyes alert & attentive.
My intrigue was derailed quickly,
upon the awareness
of angelic beings
whose drawn bows
each had the name of a fox,
with a curse mark
of damned
should they bruise
any daisy to whom
they were entrusted.

I asked the kid,
"why are you helping these children?"
His response was,

"I was one of them."

Since there was no hope for him
after his 'x' number of deportations,
he joined the street gang
to have access to helping others
in this controlled area.

He was "from there"
and understood the perils,
now he could be a point of contact
others could trust
and placed his life on the line.

Today was hot, I had a headache and heartache. I needed a break and didn't know what else to do. The team was worn—emotionally exhausted, physically exhausted, mentally and spiritually exhausted. We took a break for the afternoon and walked back across the international bridge; found a Starbucks, used the restroom and ordered a black cold brew. Then it hit me and yea, I hope it hits you too... I was able to escape and cross over in a sheer moment of "I need a break". Leaving behind all the perils and pain when I decided I had enough, when I decided I couldn't take it anymore, when I was pressed and uncomfortable.

GIVE ME A BREAK
STARBUCKS

Embarrassingly my creature comforts
die hard
but I didn't know what to do—
a bleeding heart in one hand
& in the other
a cold brew.
My rejuvenation of life came from
a cup of condensation
& dirty bean water.

I often tell people, to their surprise, that whether it's makeshift migrant camps or UN camps I always eat well when I'm with sojourners. We were speaking with a group when a woman walked over selling some empanadas—yes, I gladly purchased a few. We asked about her story and how we could pray for her; she broke down crying and told us about her children and that they were enroute but at the time she didn't know where. Often, it is the case that family members are "on their way up" and communication gets cut off for a time, or worse, indefinitely.

FILLED
WALKING ABOUT THE CAMP

A mother walks over
thinking she's just
selling empanadas:
she fills our stomachs
we fill her heart
everyone walks away
with tears
& renewed strength.

I've watched too many eyes, young and wise, too many lifted heads watching the flow of people walk freely across the international bridges. People who are looking to start life anew, to begin living, to leave the trauma and pain behind them yet they are denied the decency of humanity because politics would rather people be pawns.

UNDERFOOT
UNDER THE INTERNATIONAL BRIDGE

what happens to the psyche
of an image bearer of God
watching thousands walk by
and you are paralyzed;
not physically
but because of policy?

River banks, makeshift beds, tent city, shoeless children, muddy faces, the elements have their way with you—it was good to know help came from folks who actually cared cuz it certainly wasn't the government. The living conditions were beneath the dignity set for humanity, these environments were never meant to be experienced by people, yet here they were, here I was and there sat this five gallon bucket.

UNTITLED
SITTING IN A TENT

the irony,
pails sitting in corners
of dirt floors
read,
"always use clean water"

I returned to the migrant camp in Matamoros after some months. What most people don't know is that when the heat turns up on the political climate and the pressure of the American gauntlet increases on our Mexican neighbors everyone becomes mean and migrants are better off trekking Hades for mercy. Sojourners are treated as less than; all dignity is stripped away, they are criminalized, made to be seen as goblins under bridges, monsters looking to steal life's joy—so if there is no humanity in a person seeking asylum, then putting them in cages or barring them from any resources isn't seen as inhumane. This was one of those times. The Mexican Government was pressured by the U.S. Government to control the masses. So barbed wire fences were set up to block access to the river, the latrines and street access—people were caged like animals but even animals have PETA to aid them.

CORRIENDO
BACK OF THE CAMP

fences are being used
to keep people from
running water
while we've been
running for our lives.

A GENTLE SOUL

Meet Rosita

I stayed overnight in this tent city on the Rio Grande with the migrants. The city began to wake and cars honked as they crossed the international bridge. I could hear Rosita sweetly singing with a joy and hope that could only come from a greater source of strength.

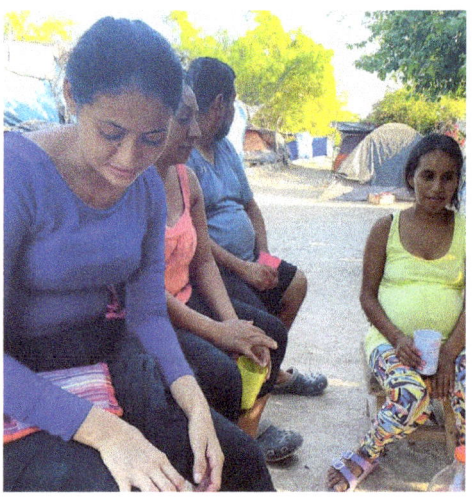

Rosita (in blue) sharing her dreams

"la campanas de la iglesia estan sonando."

Rosita's voice trails off in the wind...

A POWER HOUSE

Meet Sandra

Sandra is an inspiring example of the incredible strength and resilience that exists within humanity. Despite her treacherous 30-day journey to the border she never lost hope. Every obstacle presented only made for a new stepping stone of faith, a testament to Sandra's strong-willed spirit. She became a leader in the migrant camp, connected me to others and opened my understanding of a world broken yet beautiful.

Sandra and her girls Naomi (left) Yeimy (right)

"In the middle of the pain there's a rose."

A woman presenting her case before the man deciding her fate was confronted with disdain. I listened to her story recanted through tears—the judge's concern was how she was dressed in his courtroom, disregarding the fact that her dignity was stripped away.

SANDRA SHARING AN INTERACTION OF A WOMAN & JUDGE DURING COURT HEARINGS.

SANDRA WITH
TEARS IN HER EYES
AND A BIG SMILE

"The devil must be furious, everything he throws at us makes us laugh and fight harder."

"The first time I saw the American flag I was rushed with emotions. I desired to be on its land and upset with it because here I stand, wanting to be a part yet watching it wave from across the river as it fights against me."

Sandra looking out across the Rio Grande

I stood on the banks looking up at the white tents of immigration courts on the American side, like sails of tall ships (a waste of citizen tax dollars) our star-spangled banner waving in freedom, proud and looking good, yet I was ashamed for it was not a beacon of strength and hope but a banner like the Jolly Roger giving no quarter—Freedom was being pirated.

LET FREEDOM RING
ON THE WATER'S EDGE

I can see freedom.
I can hear freedom.
I can smell freedom,
tainted & taunting
carried off by the wind.
Cattails & trees
on the banks
of the Rio Grande
sway to its ring
cackling at our pain.

I looked out onto the street from under a tarp sheltering me from the Mexican sun, the fence had razor wire. I wasn't incarcerated and the people behind them were women and children seeking asylum, which is a human right. A woman knew I was an American citizen and interrupted my solemn moment...

PENSIVE
LOOKING THROUGH THE FENCE

I looked some razors in the face
& I don't even shave.
I looked a refugee in the face
& she asked, "are you here to save?"

This is a tough one. After so many trips and being a part of the people, gaining trust and wanting to serve in a better capacity, I asked deeper questions. Not just because of my own curiosity but because questions help to filter, questions lead to understanding, but questions can also lead to trouble—and I learned that quickly. My small team and I have seen, heard and understood some things over the years. By nature of being part of a different world, I allowed my curiosity to press into some obscure things and I pressed with questions. My original questions were never answered but I gained a new perspective, a new understanding, knowledge and wisdom. A warning to leave things alone and go about my business.

CONSEQUENCES
MAKING CONTACT

My Cartel contact
reminds me of the conduct
in which this organization runs.

If I make my move
to ask questions
in regards to their practices,
I've not only placed a price on my head
but I've set a dangerous precedent
of anxiety, arousal & suspicion
of those who come after me,
of those they may interact with
& she is already on a watch list.

Ones I've come to love,
shouldn't have to bear the burden
of my curiosities,
of my inquiries
for while a price may be named for me—
these people are priceless.

TRIGGER WARNING

*The following poem references
sexual abuse and violence.*

How do I console
the 14 year old
that was raped
by a Cartel member?

How do I fortify her mothers spirit?

How do I rebuild their dignity
set a balm on their souls
and remind them
of the love of Jesus?

All I could do
is look them
in their eyes,
listen to their stories,
allow our hearts
to meld together;
an embrace that says,
"I'm an ambassador of Christ
and The Comforter resides in me.

So, I am here,
allow me to mourn with you."

I noticed that I got more push back from border agents when I told them I was a missionary or pastor or immigration advocate than just a tourist or visiting person. We are always choosing between God and Mammon, choosing what we submit to and it permeates every aspect and engagement of life.

IDOLS
CUSTOMS & CHECKPOINTS

You can't serve both God and money
guardians of the border
accept you as a tourist
rather than a walking Jesus.

We woke up early, grabbed an Uber, headed to the bus station and took a wonderful trip to Monterrey, Mexico. It's just shy of five hours from McAllen, TX and the trek is wonderful. Watching the sun rise over the Mexican landscape was heavenly but honestly most sunrises and sunsets at the border are amazing!

DIVINE FLEX
CARRETERA 40

There's something about the glory of God
radiating over border-lands,
no true language to which we are capable
of using captures fully
the colors of impeccable
might & beauty
—
It's badass.

A VIEW FROM THE BUS ON THE WAY TO MONTERREY

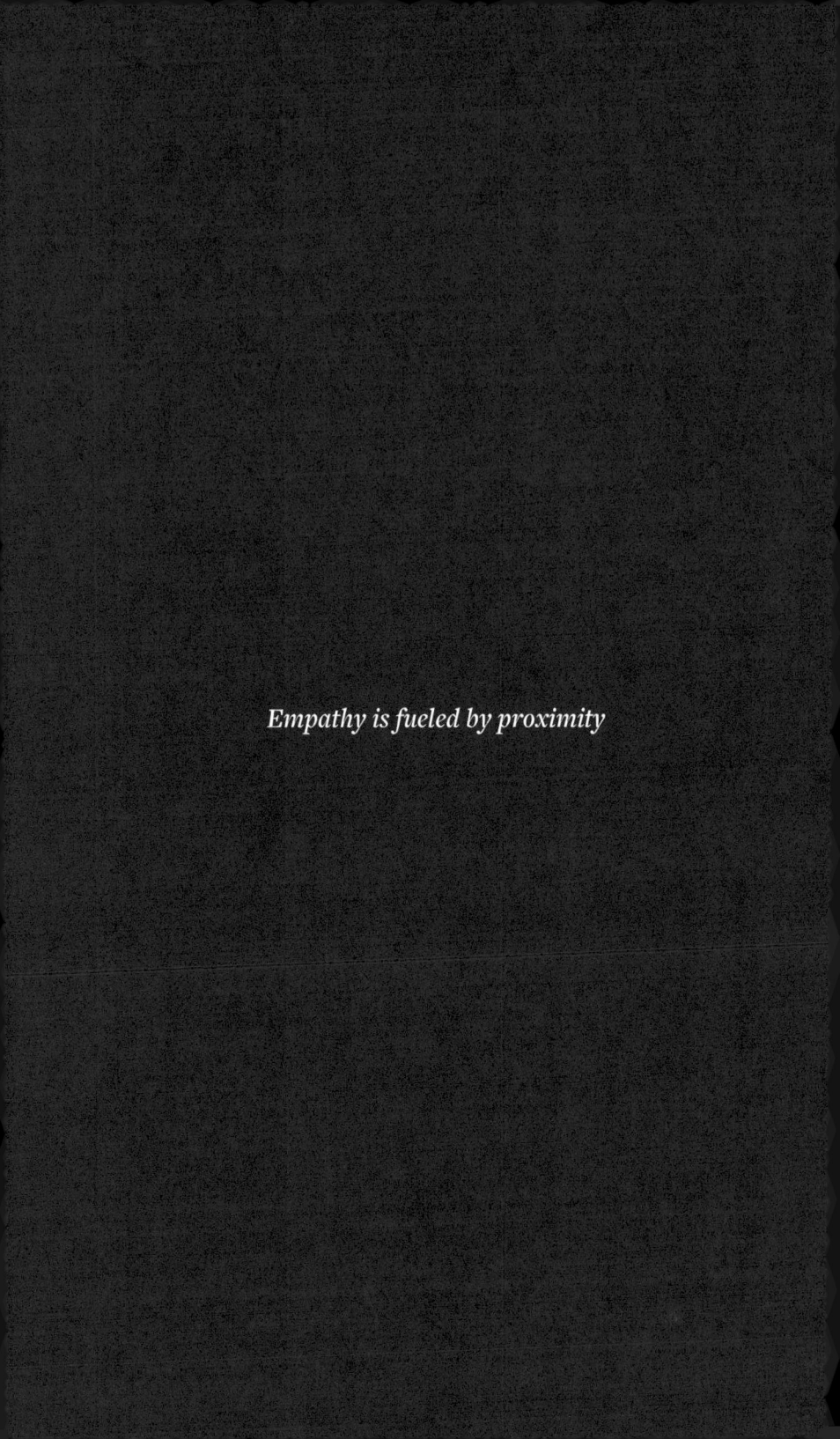

and deepens understanding.

We don't have to wait til later my dear Christian, my dear reader, you can catch and embrace glimpses of Heaven on Earth today. Too often we look to the future because we don't understand the goodness of God for today's immediate moments.

TODAY IS THE DAY

"Therefore , you should pray like this:
Our Father in Heaven,
Your name be honored as holy.
Your kingdom come
Your will be done
on earth as it is in Heaven."

Jesus brought Heaven
With all its rights & privileges
beauty & treasures
to
Earth
and too often
we are so spiritually farsighted
that we miss out on his gifts
and glimpses of our future, unified
homes.
Heaven & Earth
will
become one
but we can
taste that glory
now.

NOE: PASTOR,
BROTHER, FRIEND

"Dios no tienes nietos, solo hijos."

Truly God likes to show up in the obscure moments. This was one of those late flights with an early start; I'm tired, worn, my head's still a little foggy and I definitely haven't had enough coffee. Still in those weird hours I find that there are always God moments and conversations that almost rip the fabric of time and space allowing persons to enjoy the suspension between now and forever.

REMNANTS
TACO PALENQUE

Late nights & early mornings
—

I've learned in these quiet times
Divine moments are birthed.
A Filipino pastor encouraging your soul,
feeding your belly,
honoring your being.
Mexican Uber drivers
pulling up
engaging in
Heavenly conversations.

An indigenous Mayan woman was asked to pray over the meal and gathering in her native tongue rather than Spanish, which was her third language. I've never felt such a presence of the Almighty as when this woman shifted from anxious thought to freedom of expression; her confidence continued to build and her spirit joined with The Holy Spirit and they danced through words around that little dining room that afternoon. God is love and he is a God who listens.

PRAYER LANGUAGE
AT THE DINNER TABLE

You have never heard
a language of poetry
a song of transcendence
until you've been in the vicinity
of auditory beauty
and vibrations which reverberate
to your soul's core—
that of an indigenous woman
from Q'eqchi Mayan decent
praying to her creator
to her Love & Lord—
Jesus

                          Selah

In that moment
you dare not move
as you sense his presence
he communes with her
your soul melts
in awe & reverence
before his
compassion & tenderness.

Whether it's conversations with people in border towns or on the Rio Grande River, there is a disconnect of true conversation and unity across people. US vs Them. Migrants vs Mexicans. Politicians keep the people in fear and muddy the waters so no one is drinking something refreshing.

"BLESS YOUR HEART"

The Rio Grande
Where neighbors wave
With Southern hospitality
Yet that's where it sits,
As seeds scattered
On the soil only to be scorched
And picked away by
policy & political vultures:
Never rooting, never sprouting,
Never blooming into brotherly love
but at least we can wave.

ENJOY

THE

LANGUAGE

OF

POETRY

May the bouquet of life's stories
held within my vessel
exude a scent of Heavenly petrichor
for we are God's children
planted on Earth
to be taken and given,
transplanted and propagated,
until Eden is once again
restored.

PART

TWO

BEAUTY HEALS

I walk into the camp,
tents popped up,
heads peek around
tarps tethered to any extension available.
I see kids running,
refugees, asylum seekers,
migrants smiling.
food is being shared,
handed out of makeshift kitchens
stoves carved & molded from the earth.
The scent of latin cuisine makes you salivate.
There's beauty in the brokenness.
Pope Francis said, "beauty heals"
so I guess
with every laugh birthed out of pain,
it's a reminder that you are beautiful.

Walking the Matamoros migrant camp

A MIGRANT
ENCOURAGING ME

"Even if I don't
understand English
it doesn't matter
because the weight of
words penetrate the
heart and soul, I can
feel the weight."

PARA JASON
A SPOKEN WORD PIECE

This isn't a pretty, wrapped,
well placed package
type of story—
Jason's arms were torn shreds
puss, scabs, dried flesh.
The desert literally whooped his ass,
as he dove and fell under trees,
across the ground and onto
prickly pear cactus bushes.
His feet branded by the scorching earth.
he hobbles along sore ankles
burning calves,
tired toes holding up the weight of his body
so not to open the wounds of his heels.
"Lord, I can't die out here,
"I'm only 24 and I just started living,
my daughter needs me as a provider."

PARA JASON

And let me tell you,
his daughter is so precious
I've seen her pictures,
a beauty,
dark curly hair with clear hazel eyes
and a complexion like
that of a toasted marshmallow
you could eat her up
But
there's no work, no safe houses,
the cities are worse.
Smugglers & coyotes,
only bring you
to a place of shattered dreams.
"Oh, do it legally" you say?
Well, what can you tell me
about the process of immigration?
Jason's gotten a taste of freedom,
as he ate the dust & soil
of our borderlands.
Thirsted for our water,
arrested & deported five times
for the position to which
you & I were born into.

A position that was freely given.
When's the last time
you spent three-hundred dollars
just to set an appointment
for a visa that'll be denied

every
single
time.

You see,
a man's pockets only go so deep,
a man's hope can only stay out of reach
for so long especially when
he's got mouths to feed,
a wife & daughter of three.

Which carries more weight,
human life or legalities?

Look them in the eyes
before responding to me.

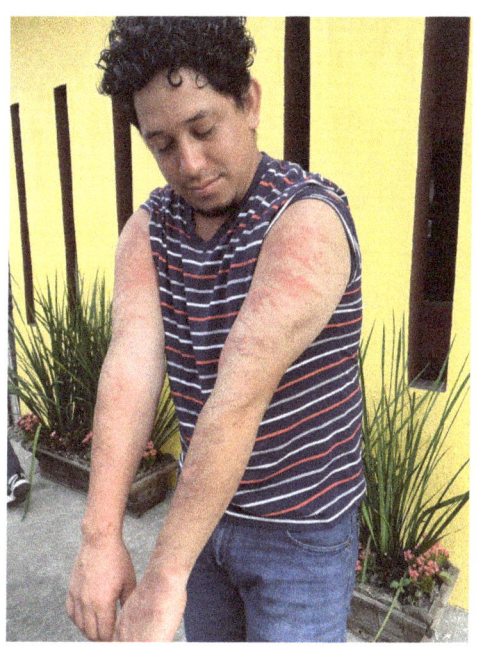
After Practice Mercy Foundation rescued him

ARROGANCE

Are we so bold and proud America
—
To think that God would
hear
The cries of mothers,
The shouts of fathers,
See
the tears of children
And
He would stay his hand?
Steady his heart,
Ignore
their calls for salvation
Because
We are mighty & good?

I'M

YELLING

IN

THIS

NEXT

ONE...

Forgive me,
but I'm feeling a bit defensive,
so I might get a little loud
at the arrogance
of people who scream
"Taco Tuesday!"
with tequila shots,
pop bottles of Corona
on Cinco de Mayo
yet have disgust at
the originating immigrants.

Now, let me set the record straight
on behalf of the Central Americans
ignorantly placed into our finite
understanding of brown skinned bodies
that trek thousands of miles of terrain,
terror-trains & risky business
to get their sons & daughters
to a better place,
a land of promise & freedom,
the home of the brave.
—

how dare we
fight wars
as Police of the World
then frown at those
who look up to US
and desire to live
with our sense of peace,
better yet privilege?

we go off to college
on prestigious trips
pretending to be hot shit
because we beat the odds,
took four years of Spanish
but can't speak a lick.

Then we turn to the
Spanish speaking orator,
and tell them to speak English
so they can get a job.

Let me school you a bit,
Mr. Protect our borders,
but will never work
the hours or positions
of those who come over.

The Mexican Government
recognizes 68 national languages
spoken within their order.
63 of which are indigenous
meaning they stem
from a peninsula reigning kingdom
we Americans love to discover—
Mayans!

Now let me tell you about
those of Aztec Blood,
whose second language is Español
but since they want to be like us
end up forgetting their indigenous roots
and trade their community
for the uniqueness of "me"!

We're so focused on self
guised as safety for securing borders
we can't see through the lens of brotherhood:
thus we sit
getting fat off the food,
drunk off the wine
we never labor for
and get mad at Robin Hood
for breaking the rules.

INHERITANCE

Stories, wine & heavenly table settings
—
These are gifts inherited by mankind
Passed down through generations.
They were shared by the Triune God
So its a right & privilege
To share in the same.

HISTORIAS

Stories build societies,
fortify communities,
create connections.
Stories tear down all strongholds
and barriers within the heart,
thus compelling warriors to drop arms
and embrace strangers as kin.

A LONE STAR CONVERSATION

He was a Texas Ranger,
leather boots with an embroidered shield.
We took trips on the wild side—
border patrol.
His insight is heavy;
taught me to spot tracks,
showed me river routes & smuggler traps.
I knew some things
but he opened my eyes to see clearer.
I processed his stories and these new experiences,
allowing for lulls in the conversations
like when we drifted down the Rio Grande.
I brought up hunting
looking to change the narrative and
engage in big bad Texas type of things.

A LONE STAR CONVERSATION

"Son, once you've hunted people for a living
the smell of blood & gunpowder changes you.
No longer do you enjoy the taste & thrill of the hunt,
I don't hunt anymore.
Many of us in law enforcement
end up turning our lips
to the glass for a different thirst
and still end up losing ourselves."

A RETIRED
TEXAS RANGER

"Most of these kids are good soldiers just following orders.

After a while you gotta ask yourself,

Can you keep on being a good soldier by just following orders?"

HURACÁN

Could it be
that hurricanes
represent the heartbreak & tears of our God?
That the magnitude of the pain He feels
washes over us as torrential rains?

Our fear,
anxiety,
burden of death
is our own doing—
Sin.

So when He says,
"Be still & know"
while the world is wasting away,
he calls us to stand
firm on his foundations
secure in his arms
and draws us together in diverse unity
to serve one another in the present
for he's taken care of eternity.

EXCHANGES

According to Christ
we're worth our weight in gold;
proved his point
when He exchanged his life for our souls.
What does a man profit to gain the world?
questions asked by The son of man.
I take a look at the exchange rates
its no wonder some of these nations be
damned—

THE HONDURIAN

Have you ever seen a grown man cry?
Fiddling with his pockets,
Looking around as he musters up the courage
to tell his story to this American.
His hope is that I can echo his words
to my fellow citizens
with a rattling force so strong
it loosens their cages!

His wife was allowed into the states
with his daughter
as the judge looked him in the eyes
and said, "but you sir can take your son back
across the border."

Yes, become furious at this statement!

Now a family is s e p a r a t e d,
A mother, a daughter
without her son and the father.

How can this pro-life nation,
police of the world
equality driven—
with an excellent Constitution
truly believe these evidences to be true?
Yet families sit unregarded
living in fear
at our doorsteps.

When will we cease to let it go any further?
and that's not the end of his story.

He sweats bullets for fear of bullets
from The Cartel;
There's a common thread in the camp
which has yet to be severed
but I digress, that's for another poem.

This Hondurian was the one
who found the body of the Guatemalan son
shot down but according to the media
"he drowned"
proofs are in the iPhone pics.

He believes he's being watched
as do others and most of these bronze bodies
won't even whisper the name, Cartel.

I laughed,
until I'm confronted for my stupidity
in shame as all the faces say,
"How can he laugh in the face of danger?
Little do they know I was just naive.

THE HONDURIAN

I took his phone for a closer look
at the shots he took

It glitches, its hot;
I know full well
this phones been hacked,
I can't tell him that.

He asks in full humility
that I not forget him
and if I could, please get his family back.

GIFTED

What do you know of hospitality?
This woman who owns nothing,
was gifted with the art of "ex nihilo":
just as the Lord created out of nothing
she uses the Spirit of Gratitude
through God's Holy Power
to call forth a table fit for kings
among us peasants.

JUGO

I was thirsty.

The heat of the Mexican sun beat down and
my energetic-mexican-friend called me over
because, "I had to hear another story" so,
I stepped into this makeshift tent store.

Upon raising my head I saw tarps hanging
from trees, a couple makeshift tables held up
with water pails and milk crates. Yesenia was
able to get her hands on some cucumbers and
citrus that morning, she was elated.

As I sat she handed me a cup.
"Here drink up, it's hot out there and you
could use something refreshing",
she says in Spanish.

This asylum seeking, cartel fleeing, former
juice bar owner, living on the river bank slum
of the US-Mexican Border with her 14 year
old daughter handed me a cup of freshly
pressed juice to quench my thirst.

At that moment I realized, I was walking in the steps of Christ. I was the least of these and she extended a moment of grace and service to care for my needs with the best she had.

My thirst was quenched, my heart was full, my spirit was humbled and I am forever left with the thought, "How is the one coming to serve being served in return?"

The simplest of tasks is
kindness to your fellow man.

"When I was thirsty
you gave me something to drink."
–Jesus

Yesenia took it one step further, she made me a drink from the first fruits she had.

Fresh pressed Jugo made by Yesenia

LEMONADE

been a long day,
heat was real,
the burden was heavy,
the screams were adhered.
media outlets showed up,
migrants rolled deep,
our squad was small
but the impact
had a long reach.

tears were shed,
hearts were shared,
testimonies flowed,
you should have heard
his, hers and their speeches—
powerful!

they raised their voices well
they held their weighted words
with poise,
and when the coordinated chaos
subsided,
the world understood our noise.

we walked through Mexican streets,
17 century bricks,
the city surely shows it's age.

strolling into a car garage
stepped up to the second floor.
I'm led into a grand restaurant
open layout,
bay windows,
with dressed for business type of people
and here I am
Feeling & looking like a wreck.

normally,
I'm not bothered,
but I just walked
off dusty roads
screaming and hollering,
With sweaty drenched brows.

no mixed drink could settle
the mix of emotions as
I see the wealth,
the arrogance,
the "je ne sais quoi" overflow.

The maître d' makes an announcement
asks for all to raise a glass
I can't raise my head,
as the cellist lowers her bow.
announcing their 30th anniversary,
families and friends cheer
"ha-ha" & "here here!"
"Young folk bring your dates"
"Families & friends today we celebrate,
our legacy, our success, your patronage"

LEMONADE

the musicians play,
the singer belts out some Sinatra,
finishing with a
smooth Spanish bellow,
"The record shows
I took the blows
and did it my way!"

am I sitting in the capital
of the Hunger Games?
ate half my food,
as all I could do
was look past shadowy figures
overlooking the immigration camp
as if it didn't exist.
where am I?
all I wanted was some lemonade.

QUESTION

Are we not a nation of immigrants?
People forcibly embraced
by this stolen land
held hostage by its hospitality—
unhealed trauma & pain.
Yes, we've grown passed it
like most adults w/ underlying daddy issues
only to trip over the proverbial,
"Dust under the rug" every now & then.

Are we not a nation of immigrants?
With descendants
now living out their forefathers
unseen legacies
good, bad & disastrous?

Are we not Nations of immigrants?
Refugees fleeing the war against God
instigated by
humanity's patriarch Adam & matriarch Eve,
who were cast from Eden
to migrate west
as sojourners on Earth
until one day
Heaven's hospitality would embrace
their children once again?

WOULD WE COMMIT?

Oh, that we would commit to humanity—
A people of one land, Pangea.
the breaking of this very soil
has broken our souls,
the only way to mend our hearts
is with the breaking of bread,
making amends
across tribes, people groups & borders.

DOG & HORSE SHOW

military checkpoints
drug sniffing dogs
honestly it's all a show
for the viewers
more likes,
more "ohs and ahs",
more news for y'all
to say, "look at all those bad guys."
I've read the comment sections
I've seen the blogs
I've spoken with the people
striving to beat the odds.
at the end of the day
we'll never take responsibility
we'll never take the loss
of knowing all the trafficked goods
and paraphernalia was really
all of ours.

ADVENTURE & RISK

I never want my sense of adventure
and need for calculated risk
to be filled by the plight
of someone else's disadvantaged life.
Missions and trips to be with
the "least of these"
should never satisfy our need
for seeing the world & exotic-other
but should always complete the high call
to bring hope, practice mercy
and answer the question,
"why are you here?!" with, "Jesus sent me".

THE ROAR OF HEAVEN

The scriptures speak of prayers
lifting before the throne as incense.
that the Holy Spirit in all his wonder
carry's our praise & petitions in golden bowls.
I tell you now that Heaven rings
with the reverberations
of a thousand gongs
as the voice of God
echoes in his saints
and it is magnificent!
In this moment
darkness is displaced
with the roar of his voice—
women of Mayan & Aztec decent
speak in their native tongues,
a chorus to which the good Lord joins,
and as the psalm speaks of God
singing over his people
here we are covered,
wavelengths from earth
resonando en los patios del Cielo.

TREASURED TALES

Strangers in a plane
ladies of 21
young and fun
ready to take on the world.
They're Cali bound
and bound to take in what life offers,
at least that's what they tell me.
It's awesome, sharing stories—
stories connect strangers
and although I'm heading further south
here we are forever tethered because of the
exchange of smiles:
social currency
with more weight than any monetary value.
It's the reason that oral traditions,
folklore and tales have been
written and passed down through generations,
treasured tales of old,
reminders that stories elevate all who listen
and all who would tell a tale of wonders.

SANTA MUERTE

I looked at death in the face—
well, not truly her
but an idol in her name and honor
standing about 3 foot short,
we both looked into each others eyes
hers were dark & hollow
mine are dark & full.
I crossed the street bringing with me
Hope, Life, Mercy;
she stood there
deaf, dumb and blind—
I'll see her thrown in Hell,
while I'm in Heaven casting crowns.

WITNESS

I've seen the gates,
I've heard the stories,
I've witnessed the dust ridden faces
washed in tears—
I've been honored to be loved,
I've been honored to love
and hold the faces
of people our Lord Jesus holds dear.

MIGRANTS BEING DEPORTED BY U.S. BORDER PATROL

MIRANDO

rich or poor
one day we will all look
upon the mountain of God
with no distinction of persons

DISTANCE

It's hard to fathom
that we would defend
a plot of land
over a fellow man—
we are
creatures with unique compositions;
of which I'm told
have some base characteristics of stars
and as much as they are enamored
with awe-inspiring oculus
I've only ever beheld them
but humans,
humans I've heard & held.
Mothers, fathers, sisters, brothers
numbering that of the Earth's sandy shores
numbering that of the starry hosts yet
we are greater than those distant orbs
forever out of arm's reach but for those
that are at our doors we treat with less dignity
than the distant reverence of unknown bodies
only brought near by Hubble & James-Webb.

ALWAYS NEAR

I've seen the ends of the earth
I've witnessed the lineages of kings
I've walked among the reeds
spoken by God's decree
separating men from dreams.
I've seen the hand of Heaven
lay gently upon a women's face,
while strangling the darkness
lurking about to seal her fate.
I've sensed the heart of God
I've heard his voice too
and in both instances
I've felt fear,
for no truer moment rocks your world
when known is the distance between his arms
and our tears—
proving he is always near.

Looking southwest to the wilderness

PEACE BE WITH YOU & PEACE I LEAVE WITH YOU

Five Mexican pesos
To a U.S. quarter.
That's what the sign reads
As I walk across the border.
I've inherited the lives of Central Americans
And this is one situation
Where I can't walk in their shoes—
Hell, they don't even own some.

As I fight the tears
To recite their narratives,
Emotions of anxiety & fear;
The hope is that my writing
Will respect & honor them.
The faces whose names
Are now wrinkles in my mind,
A beat in my heart
A song in my soul.

I don't know
If we'll ever meet again
But all they had they gave
And the last of what they spoke
Will last
Because I am passing these stories down to you.
Will you do the same?

MY FINAL REPORT

When I step onto eternity
And into the courts of praise.
I will confidently tell the king,
"I've shown them the way!"

And when he asks of their provisions,
From a bowed knee I'll say,
"You see sir, I've given all that I can
So please forgive the embarrassment of
being naked before the son of man."

Carrying donations and goods into the migrant camp

SHOT ON IPHONE

Mirando —— p. 157

Underfoot —— p. 62

Self Destruction —— p. 44

Yeimy (Jamie) —— p. 38

Hospitality —— p. 50

Peace be with You & Peace I Leave with You —— p. 159

ACKNOWLEDGMENTS

In the journey of bringing this book to life, I have been blessed to cross paths with a multitude of incredible individuals whose contributions, support, and presence have been invaluable. This endeavor would not have been possible without the unwavering love, encouragement, and strength provided by those who have stood in my corner.

First and foremost, to my beloved wife, Sarah Davis—you are the cornerstone of my freedom of expression and being myself. A source of gusto that empowers me to embrace the adventures that God has scripted for my life. Your unyielding support has allowed me to embark on this literary journey, and your love and care have infused each page with a fragrance of life's beauty. Without you, this story would be incomplete and these stories would not be shared.

To Alma Ruth, whose open heart and ministry have taught me the profound significance of offering shelter to strangers and being a ministry of presence in the lives of others. Your kindness and example have enriched my understanding of empathy and compassion especially towards the sojourner.

Sandra Andrade, your introduction to a world of depth, community, and richness has broadened my horizons in ways I could never have fathomed. Your connection has been a beacon of growth, faith, resilience and understanding.

Elizabeth Bell, your friendship and partnership on this writing odyssey has been an absolute joy. Your ability to nurture my wild ideas and transform them into tangible reality is a gift beyond measure.

To Will McCorkle, your simple question—*"will you go and see?"*—became a catalyst for leaps of faith and new horizons. Your courage to ask has led to countless extraordinary experiences.

Caeli Faisst, your dedication to editing my poetry with unapologetic honesty has refined my craft and made these words all the more meaningful. Your truths, no matter how hard, have been a guidepost toward improvement.

Falando Jones, your sharing in my life's journey has been a testament to the power of Kingdom mindedness. Your platform and connections have cleared logistical hurdles and allowed me to reach my destinations with ease.

Dana Pettus, your commitment to proofreading and correcting my grammar, even babysitting so the team could meet, speaks volumes about your dedication to this project's success.

Terrance P. Elmore, your persistent encouragement and nudges have pushed me beyond my comfort zones to achieve my goals. Your unwavering belief in my abilities has been a driving force.

Marcus Amaker, your early recognition of my poetic talents planted a seed of creativity that has blossomed into this collection. Your words of encouragement have been a constant source of inspiration.

And to the entire G&T Crew, your late nights of camaraderie, laughter, tears, and shared meals have given me strength and support beyond words. Your collective wisdom and encouragement have molded me into a better human, and your unwavering push to "get this done" has fueled the realization of this dream.

To each of you, I extend my deepest gratitude. Your contributions, whether small or monumental, have woven together the fabric of this book, making it a reflection of the love, friendship, and shared experiences that define our lives.

Inspiring dignity with grit and grace,
Tethered Wrds